SOUTH CAROLINA

BY EMILY ROSE OACHS

BELLWETHER MEDIA • MINNEAPOLIS, MN

Blastoff! Discovery launches a new mission: reading to learn. Filled with facts and features, each book offers you an exciting new world to explore!

BLASTOFF! UNIVERSE

GRADE K

GRADES 1-3

GRADE 4

This edition first published in 2022 by Bellwether Media, Inc.

No part of this publication may be reproduced in whole or in part without written permission of the publisher.
For information regarding permission, write to Bellwether Media, Inc.,
Attention: Permissions Department,
6012 Blue Circle Drive, Minnetonka, MN 55343.

Library of Congress Cataloging-in-Publication Data

Names: Oachs, Emily Rose, author.
Title: South Carolina / by Emily Rose Oachs.
Description: Minneapolis, MN : Bellwether Media, Inc., 2022. |
    Series: Blastoff! Discovery: State profiles | Includes bibliographical
    references and index. | Audience: Ages 7-13 | Audience: Grades
    4-6 | Summary: "Engaging images accompany information about
    South Carolina. The combination of high-interest subject matter and
    narrative text is intended for students in grades 3 through 8"–
    Provided by publisher.
Identifiers: LCCN 2021020878 (print) | LCCN 2021020879 (ebook)
    | ISBN 9781644873465 (library binding) |
    ISBN 9781648341892 (ebook)
Subjects: LCSH: South Carolina–Juvenile literature.
Classification: LCC F269.3 .O23 2022 (print) | LCC F269.3 (ebook)
    | DDC 975.7–dc23
LC record available at https://lccn.loc.gov/2021020878
LC ebook record available at https://lccn.loc.gov/2021020879

Editor: Betsy Rathburn   Designer: Andrea Schneider

Printed in the United States of America, North Mankato, MN.

TABLE OF CONTENTS

TABLE ROCK MOUNTAIN

TABLE ROCK MOUNTAIN
TABLE ROCK STATE PARK

A pair of hikers looks up at the tall, flat-topped
Table Rock Mountain. It rises from a thick blanket of oak
and hickory trees. The hikers start along the trail. It soon
grows steep. The hikers spot large boulders among the trees.

CONGAREE NATIONAL PARK

FORT SUMTER AND FORT MOULTRIE NATIONAL HISTORIC PARK

MIDDLETON PLACE

MYRTLE BEACH

After a few hours, the forest opens. The hikers have reached the top of Table Rock. They are more than 3,000 feet (914 meters) above sea level! The hikers carefully approach the mountain's edge. They gaze at the blue lake in the valley below them. The Blue Ridge Mountains stretch into the distance. Welcome to South Carolina!

TENNESSEE

South Carolina is a small state in the southeastern United States. It is shaped like a triangle. It spreads across 32,020 square miles (82,931 square kilometers). At South Carolina's center stands its capital, Columbia. Its largest city, Charleston, sits on the Atlantic Coast.

South Carolina touches two other states. North Carolina is to the north. Georgia lies to the southwest. Eastern South Carolina borders the Atlantic Ocean for 187 miles (301 kilometers). Many islands also stand off the coast.

GEORGIA

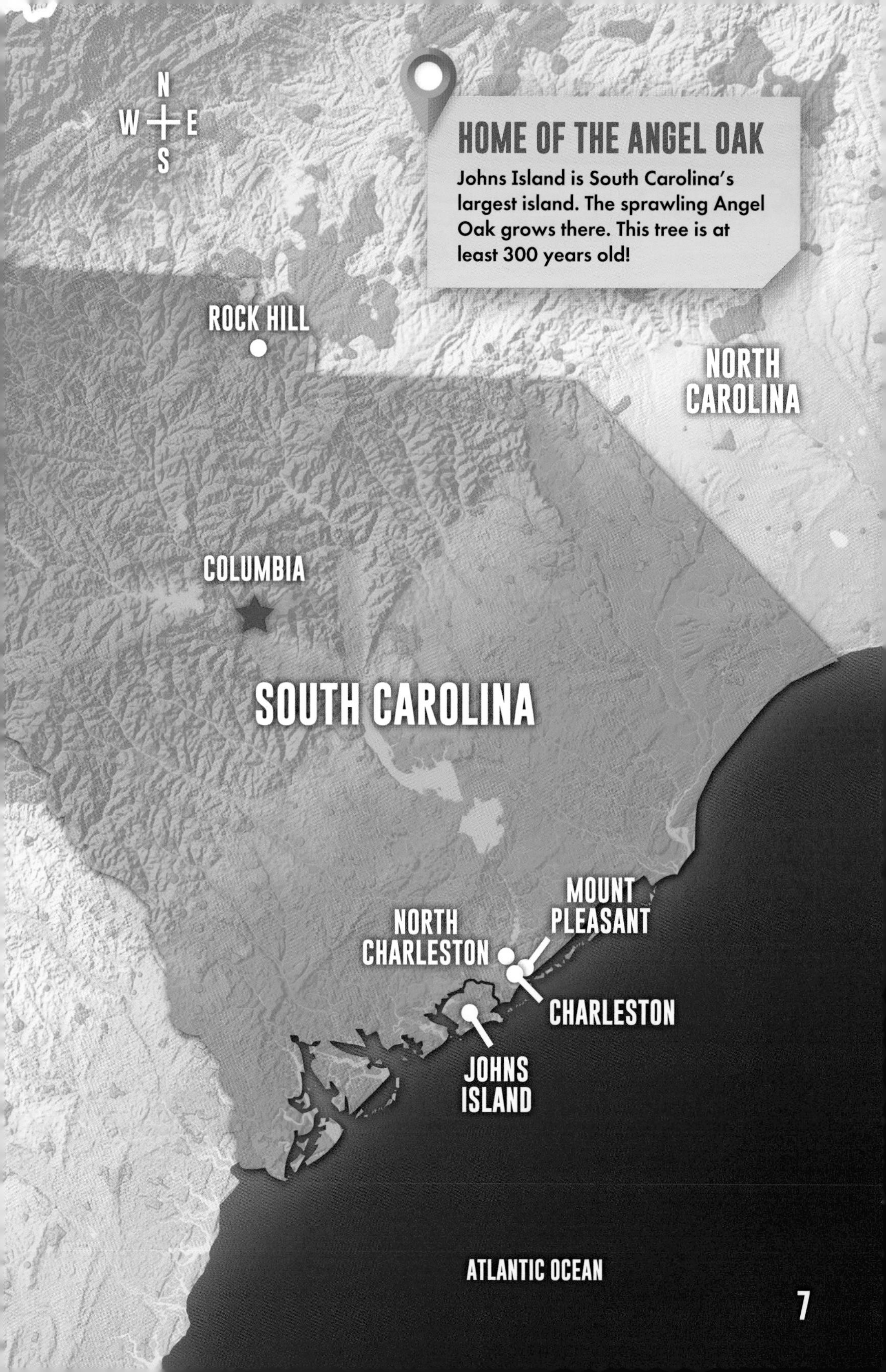

N
W + E
S

HOME OF THE ANGEL OAK

Johns Island is South Carolina's largest island. The sprawling Angel Oak grows there. This tree is at least 300 years old!

ROCK HILL

NORTH CAROLINA

COLUMBIA

SOUTH CAROLINA

MOUNT PLEASANT

NORTH CHARLESTON

CHARLESTON

JOHNS ISLAND

ATLANTIC OCEAN

7

REVOLUTIONARY WAR

People first came to South Carolina about 12,000 years ago. In time, the Congaree, Catawba, and other Native American tribes called the area home. The Spanish arrived in 1521. By 1670, the region was an English colony. The English lost control after the Revolutionary War ended in 1783. Five years later, South Carolina became the eighth U.S. state.

From early on, slavery was important to South Carolina. Thousands of Africans were forced to work on large **plantations** for hundreds of years. Starting in 1861, South Carolina fought with the **Confederacy** during the **Civil War**. The war ended in 1865, and slavery was outlawed. South Carolina rejoined the U.S. three years later.

NATIVE PEOPLES OF SOUTH CAROLINA

BEAVER CREEK

- Original lands along the Edisto River
- Around 2,000 members in South Carolina today

CATAWBA

- Original lands in South Carolina's Piedmont region
- More than 3,300 members in South Carolina today

WACCAMAW

- Original lands along the Waccamaw River
- Around 275 members in South Carolina today

PEE DEE

- Original lands along the Pee Dee River
- Two Pee Dee tribes in South Carolina
- Less than 150 members in South Carolina today

LANDSCAPE AND CLIMATE

The Atlantic Coastal **Plain** covers more than half of South Carolina. The lowlands along the coast are filled with swamps and rivers. Farther inland, forests and rolling hills cover the landscape. Then the land rises into the high, hilly Piedmont region. The hills climb to the forested Blue Ridge Mountains in the state's northwestern corner. There, Sassafras Mountain is South Carolina's highest point.

SASSAFRAS MOUNTAIN

N
W — E
S

- ATLANTIC COASTAL PLAIN
- PIEDMONT
- BLUE RIDGE MOUNTAINS

SWAMP
ATLANTIC COASTAL PLAIN

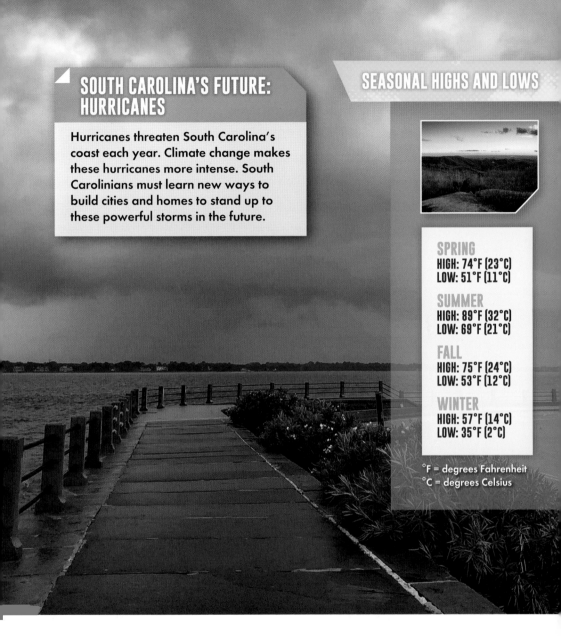

SOUTH CAROLINA'S FUTURE: HURRICANES

Hurricanes threaten South Carolina's coast each year. Climate change makes these hurricanes more intense. South Carolinians must learn new ways to build cities and homes to stand up to these powerful storms in the future.

SEASONAL HIGHS AND LOWS

SPRING
HIGH: 74°F (23°C)
LOW: 51°F (11°C)

SUMMER
HIGH: 89°F (32°C)
LOW: 69°F (21°C)

FALL
HIGH: 75°F (24°C)
LOW: 53°F (12°C)

WINTER
HIGH: 57°F (14°C)
LOW: 35°F (2°C)

°F = degrees Fahrenheit
°C = degrees Celsius

South Carolina's summers are hot and **humid**. Rainy weather and thunderstorms are common. Winters are mild. Violent **hurricanes** may strike between May and November each year.

BLACK BEAR

In the Blue Ridge Mountains, black bears sniff out meals of nuts and berries. Along rivers and creeks, muskrats hide in their dens from snakes and hawks. White-tailed deer dart through forests to escape hungry bobcats. Off the coast, sand tiger sharks hunt for fish, rays, and squid along the ocean floor.

In South Carolina's swampy wetlands, American alligators wait to attack frogs, birds, and other prey. Egrets wade in the shallow waters. Cottonmouths and eastern coral snakes slither after lizards, fish, and other prey.

SAND TIGER SHARK

AMERICAN ALLIGATOR

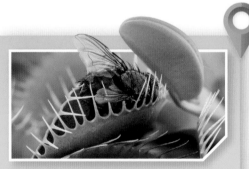

INSECT-EATING PLANT

Venus flytraps live in South Carolina's wetlands. These plants catch insects for food!

GREAT WHITE EGRET

EASTERN CORAL SNAKE

Life Span: up to 7 years
Status: least concern

eastern coral snake range = ▪

LEAST CONCERN	NEAR THREATENED	VULNERABLE	ENDANGERED	CRITICALLY ENDANGERED	EXTINCT IN THE WILD	EXTINCT

South Carolina is home to more than 5 million people. Most live in cities. The state's largest cities are Charleston, Columbia, North Charleston, and Mount Pleasant.

MOUNT PLEASANT

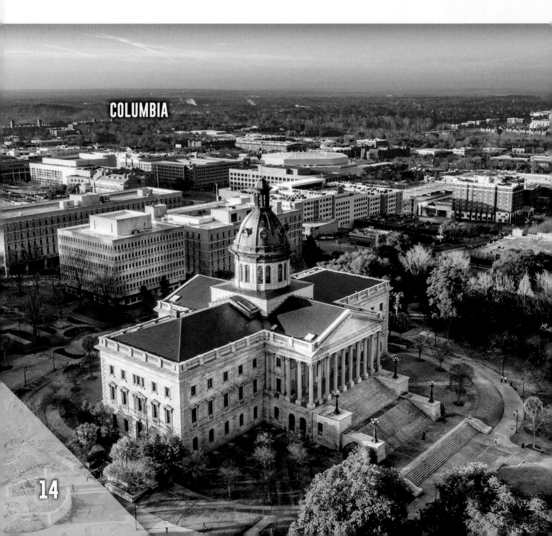

COLUMBIA

FAMOUS SOUTH CAROLINIAN

Name: Chadwick Boseman
Born: November 29, 1976
Died: August 28, 2020
Hometown: Anderson, South Carolina
Famous For: Actor famous for his roles as Jackie Robinson in *42*, James Brown in *Get on Up*, and T'Challa in *Black Panther* and other Marvel films

About 2 out of 3 South Carolinians have European **ancestry**. Black or African Americans make up the state's second-largest group. South Carolina is also home to smaller numbers of Hispanic Americans and Asian Americans. A small population of Native Americans also call South Carolina home. A growing number of **immigrants** are settling in South Carolina. Many come from Mexico, India, or Honduras.

CHARLESTON HARBOR

Charleston sits at the edge of Charleston Harbor. English **settlers** founded the city in 1670. Because of its location, it soon became a key port. It was also the center of the Atlantic slave trade. On nearby plantations, landowners forced **enslaved** people to grow rice, **indigo**, and cotton.

THE OLDEST CITY

Charleston is South Carolina's oldest city. More than 70 buildings built before the Revolutionary War still stand in Charleston today!

Today, Charleston is a lively city rich with history. Since 1807, vendors at the Charleston City Market have sold food and art. The market is especially known for its woven baskets. People browse paintings and sculptures at the Gibbes Museum of Art. The historic Dock Street Theater draws crowds to its live performances. Riley Waterfront Park is a popular place for oceanside strolls.

CHARLESTON CITY
MARKET

INDUSTRY

BMW MANUFACTURING FACILITY GREER

SOUTH CAROLINA'S FUTURE: TEACHER SHORTAGES

South Carolina's schools have been facing teacher shortages. This leads to larger class sizes and overworked teachers. It also makes learning more difficult. South Carolina needs to solve the problem so that students get the help they need in school.

Farming was the most important industry during South Carolina's early days. Slaves grew rice, cotton, and other crops on the state's many farms. There are fewer farms today. Many grow corn, cotton, or soybeans. **Manufacturing** is also important. Fabric and lumber are key products. Aircraft, cars, and medical equipment are also made in South Carolina.

Most South Carolinians have **service jobs**. They work in hospitals, schools, and libraries. They may also work in **tourism**. Many people in tourism work at hotels and restaurants.

INVENTED IN SOUTH CAROLINA

VERTICAL FILING CABINET

Date Invented: late 1800s

Inventor: Edwin Seibels

COTTON CHOPPER

Date Invented: 1894

Inventor: George Washington Murray

3-D PRINTING TECHNIQUE

Date Invented: 1983

Inventors: Charles Hull, 3D Systems

FROGMORE STEW

South Carolina is famous for its barbecue. Pork and beef are cooked over low heat for hours to make tender, flavorful meat. The meat is often topped with a mustard barbecue sauce. South Carolinians often serve barbecue with rice and a mixture of vegetables and ground meat called hash.

Many meals include fresh seafood. Cooks serve shrimp over boiled cornmeal called grits. Frogmore stew is made with shrimp, crab, and vegetables. Diners also enjoy seafood with fried cornmeal balls called hushpuppies. Favorite desserts include peach cobbler and pie.

SHRIMP AND GRITS

HUSHPUPPIES

PEACH COBBLER

4 SERVINGS

Have an adult help you make this popular dessert!

INGREDIENTS

1/2 cup butter
1 cup all-purpose flour
1/2 teaspoon salt

1 3/4 cups sugar, divided
3 teaspoons baking powder

1 cup milk
3 cups peeled and sliced peaches

DIRECTIONS

1. Preheat the oven to 350 degrees Fahrenheit (177 degrees Celsius).

2. Melt the butter. Pour into a shallow baking pan or casserole dish.

3. Add the flour, salt, 1 cup sugar, baking powder, and milk to a medium bowl. Stir to combine.

4. Pour the flour mixture into the baking pan over the butter. Spread evenly across the butter. This will form the cobbler's bottom crust.

5. In a separate bowl, mix the peaches and 3/4 cup sugar together.

6. Pour the peaches over the flour mixture. Spread evenly but do not stir with the flour mixture.

7. Bake for 45 minutes. Enjoy with vanilla ice cream!

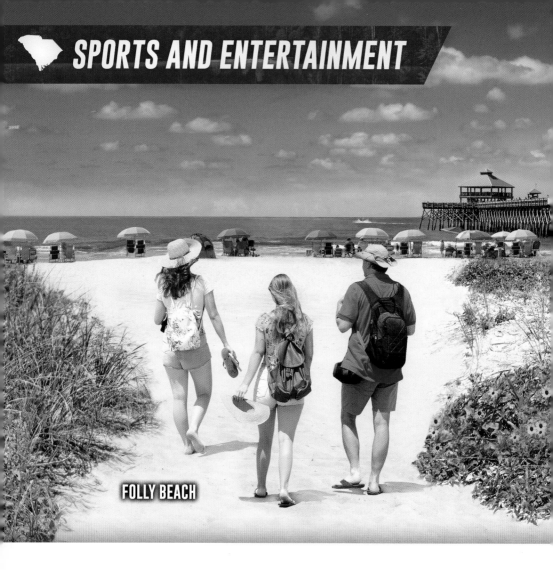

FOLLY BEACH

Many South Carolinians root for college sports teams. Clemson University Tigers games draw football fans. The South Carolina Gamecocks women's basketball team is often among the best in the nation! South Carolina also offers many outdoor activities. Beaches, gardens, and trails are popular. Fishing is common throughout the state's lakes, rivers, and coastline.

Music is also important to South Carolina. Early jazz and **bluegrass** have roots there. Live concerts of these musical styles are popular. In major cities, theater performances also draw crowds.

BIRD-WATCHING

South Carolina's wilderness draws many bird-watchers. More than 400 types of birds live across the state. Bird-watchers love scanning the skies for roseate spoonbills, pileated woodpeckers, and scarlet tanagers!

NOTABLE SPORTS TEAM

Clemson University Tigers
Sport: National Collegiate Athletic Association football
Started: 1896
Place of Play: Memorial Stadium

Each Memorial Day weekend, Greenville hosts Gallabrae. Colorful parades, kilts, and bagpipe music bring Scottish **traditions** to the city. There are also contests for throwing axes and telephone poles! In May and June, Charleston fills with art lovers for the Spoleto Festival. For 17 days, the city bursts with music, art, and dance performances.

SPOLETO FESTIVAL

SWEETGRASS
FESTIVAL

In July, Mount Pleasant's Sweetgrass Festival celebrates the Gullah people. People gather to eat Gullah food, listen to music, and browse traditional sweetgrass baskets. Throughout the year, South Carolinians have a lot to celebrate!

OODLES OF OYSTERS

In January, the Lowcountry Oyster Festival comes to Mount Pleasant. More than 80,000 pounds (36,287 kilograms) of oysters help make it the world's biggest oyster festival!

1521

The first known Spanish explorers arrive in South Carolina

1775

The first of more than 200 Revolutionary War battles in South Carolina takes place

1670

The English build their first settlement in South Carolina near present-day Charleston

1788

South Carolina becomes the 8th state

1865
The Confederacy loses the Civil War, freeing 400,000 enslaved people in South Carolina

2003
Congaree National Park is established

2020
A monument honoring a pro-slavery South Carolinian is removed in Charleston

1993
The federal government officially recognizes the Catawba tribe

1860
South Carolina becomes the first of 11 states to join the Confederacy

2011
Nikki Haley is elected the first female governor of South Carolina

Nickname: The Palmetto State

Motto: *Dum Spiro Spero* (While I Breathe, I Hope)

Date of Statehood: May 23, 1788 (the 8th state)

Capital City: Columbia ★

Other Major Cities: Charleston, North Charleston, Mount Pleasant, Rock Hill

Area: 32,020 square miles (82,931 square kilometers); South Carolina is the 40th largest state.

Population

5,118,425
(2020)

STATE FLAG

South Carolina's flag is blue with a white crescent in the upper left corner. A white palmetto tree stands in the center. The flag is based on the flags carried by South Carolinian soldiers during the Revolutionary War. Its blue color came from soldiers' uniforms. The crescent shape appeared on their hats. The palmetto tree stands for the palmetto logs that protected a South Carolinian fort during the war.

INDUSTRY

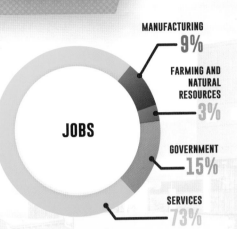

MANUFACTURING
9%

FARMING AND
NATURAL
RESOURCES
3%

GOVERNMENT
15%

SERVICES
73%

JOBS

Main Exports

vehicles

chemicals

machinery

plastics and
rubber

computers and
electronics

Natural Resources
forests, rivers, clay, sand,
vermiculite, mica

GOVERNMENT

Federal Government

7 | **2**
REPRESENTATIVES | SENATORS

9
ELECTORAL
VOTES

SC

USA

State Government

124 | **46**
REPRESENTATIVES | SENATORS

STATE SYMBOLS

STATE BIRD
CAROLINA WREN

STATE ANIMAL
WHITE-TAILED DEER

STATE FLOWER
YELLOW JESSAMINE

STATE TREE
SABAL PALMETTO

GLOSSARY

ancestry—a person's ancestors; ancestors are relatives who lived long ago.

bluegrass—a style of music played on string instruments; bluegrass began in the southern Appalachian region of the United States.

Civil War—a war between the Northern (Union) and Southern (Confederate) states that lasted from 1861 to 1865

colony—a distant territory which is under the control of another nation

Confederacy—the group of southern states that formed a new country in the early 1860s; the Confederacy fought against the Northern states during the Civil War.

enslaved—to be considered property and forced to work for no pay

humid—having a lot of moisture in the air

hurricanes—storms formed in the tropics that have violent winds and often have rain and lightning

immigrants—people who move to a new country

indigo—a plant used to create dark blue dye

manufacturing—a field of work in which people use machines to make products

plain—a large area of flat land

plantations—large farms that grow coffee, cotton, rubber, or other crops; plantations are mainly found in warm climates.

Revolutionary War—the war from 1775 to 1783 in which the United States fought for independence from Great Britain

service jobs—jobs that perform tasks for people or businesses

settlers—people who move to live in a new, undeveloped region

tourism—the business of people traveling to visit other places

traditions—customs, ideas, or beliefs handed down from one generation to the next

TO LEARN MORE

AT THE LIBRARY

DK. *The Civil War Visual Encyclopedia*. New York, N.Y.: DK Publishing, 2021.

Somervill, Barbara A. *South Carolina*. North Mankato, Minn.: Children's Press, 2019.

Tieck, Sarah. *South Carolina*. Minneapolis, Minn.: Abdo Publishing, 2020.

ON THE WEB

FACTSURFER

Factsurfer.com gives you a safe, fun way to find more information.

1. Go to www.factsurfer.com.

2. Enter "South Carolina" into the search box and click 🔍.

3. Select your book cover to see a list of related content.

INDEX

The images in this book are reproduced through the courtesy of: Kevin Ruck, front cover, pp. 2–3, 14 (Columbia), 26–27, 28–29, 30–31, 32; WilleeCole Photography, p. 3 (white-tailed deer); Jon Lovette / Alamy Stock Photo, pp. 4–5 (Table Rock Mountain); NatalieBuzzyBee, p. 5 (Congaree National Park); meunierd, p. 5 (Fort Sumter and Fort Moultrie National Historic Park, Middleton Place); Sean Pavone, pp. 5 (Myrtle Beach), 16 (oldest city); North Wind Picture Archives/ Alamy, pp. 8 (Revolutionary War), 26 (1775); Simplyphotos, p. 9; Paul Briden, p. 10 (swamp); Jerry Coli, p. 11; Wirestock Creators, p. 11 (inset); Kuttelvaserova Stuchelova, p. 12 (Venus flytrap); Dolores M. Harvey, p. 12 (black bear); Valeri Potapova, p. 12 (sand tiger shark); Juan Gracia, p. 12 (American alligator); Bildagentur Zoonar GmbH, p. 12 (great white egret); Liz Weber, p. 13 (eastern coral snake); elvisvaughn, p. 14 (Mount Pleasant); Moviestore Collection Ltd/ Alamy, p. 15 (Black Panther); Cubankite, p. 15 (Chadwick Boseman); jdross75, p. 16 (Charleston Harbor); f11photo, p. 17 (Charleston City Market); REUTERS/ Alamy, p. 18 (BMW manufacturing facility); Cavan-Images, pp. 19 (tourism), 27 (2003); Denton Rumsey, p. 19 (field background); Valentina Razumova, p. 19 (cotton chopper); Cigdem Simsek/ Alamy, p. 19 (3-D printing technique); Hurst Photo, p. 19 (filing cabinet); Engineer studio, p. 19 (military submarine); Panagiotis Kyriakos/ Alamy, p. 20 (frogmore stew); Brent Hofacker, p. 21 (shrimp and grits); Karen Culp, p. 21 (hushpuppies); fetrinka, p. 21 (peaches); iyd39, p. 21 (cobbler); Margaret.Wiktor, p. 22 (Folly Beach); Bonnie Taylor Barry, p. 23 (roseate spoonbill); Cal Sport Media/ Alamy, p. 23 (Clemson University Tigers); Mtsaride, p. 23 (football); Andy Murphy/ Alamy, p. 25 (Spoleto Festival); Richard Ellis/ Alamy, p. 25 (Sweetgrass Festival); Spayder pauk_79, p. 25 (oysters); Andrey Lobachev, p. 26 (1788); Millenius, p. 28 (flag); Danita Delimont, p. 29 (Carolina wren); Jim Cumming, p. 29 (white-tailed deer); fiz_zero, p. 29 (yellow jessamine); Thomas Barrat, p. 29 (sabal palmetto); JeniFoto, p. 31 (sweet tea).